Picture the Past
Life in a
HOPI VILLAGE

Sally Senzell Isaacs

Heinemann Library
Chicago, Illinois

© 2001 Reed Educational & Professional Publishing
Published by Heinemann Library,
an imprint of Reed Educational & Professional Publishing,
Chicago, Illinois

Customer Service 888-454-2279
Visit our website at www.heinemannlibrary.com

Produced for Heinemann Library by
  Bender Richardson White.
Editor: Lionel Bender
Designer: Ben White
Picture Researcher: Cathy Stastny
Media Conversion and Typesetting: MW Graphics
Production Controller: Kim Richardson

04 03 02
10 9 8 7 6 5 4 3

Printed in Hong Kong

Library of Congress Cataloging-in-Publication Data.
Isaacs, Sally Senzell, 1950–
    Life in a Hopi village / Sally Senzell Isaacs.
      p. cm. – (Picture the past)
    Includes bibliographical references and index.
Summary: Introduces life in a Hopi village in seventeenth-
century Arizona, discussing the homes, families and clans,
food, clothing, beliefs, and entertainment.

      ISBN 1-57572-314-X

1. Hopi Indians-Juvenile literature. (1. Hopi Indians-Social
life and customs. 2. Indians of North America-Arizona-
Social life and customs.) I. Title.

E99.H7 173 2000
979.1'0049745-dc21

                                          00-020646

Special thanks to Mike Carpenter, Scott Westerfield, and
Tristan Boyer Binns at Heinemann Library for editorial and
design guidance and direction.

Acknowledgments
The producers and publishers are grateful to the
following for permission to reproduce copyright material:
The Bridgeman Art Library/Private Collection.
Corbis: Corbis, pages 8, 11, 15, 16, 24, 28; Tom Bean,
page 19; Larry Neubauer, pages 6-7; Bob Rowan/
Progressive Image, pages 22, 23, 27; Underwood and
Underwood, pages 10, 14. Peter Newark's American
Pictures, pages 1, 3, 12, 13, 20, 21, 26. North Wind
Pictures, page 30.
Cover photograph: Corbis/Underwood and Underwood.

Every effort has been made to contact copyright holders
of any material reproduced in this book. Omissions will
be rectified in subsequent printings if notice is given to
the publisher.

Illustrations by John James.
Map by Stefan Chabluk.
Cover make-up: Mike Pilley, Pelican Graphics.

Note to the Reader
Some words are shown in bold, **like this**.
You can find out what they mean by looking in the
glossary.

ABOUT THIS BOOK

This book tells about life in a
Hopi village from 1630 to 1700.
Hopi villages were located in
what we now call Arizona.
The Hopi are Native Americans,
the first people to live on the
continent. We have illustrated
the book with photographs of
Hopi taken in the last 100 years.
There are about 8,000 Hopi alive
today, and many continue to
follow the customs, traditions, and
religious beliefs of their ancestors.
We also include artists' ideas of
how the Hopi lived in the 1600s.

The Consultant
Diane Smolinski has years of experience
interpreting standards documents and
putting them into practice in fourth and
fifth grade classrooms.

The Author
Sally Senzell Isaacs is a professional writer
and editor of nonfiction books for children.
She graduated from Indiana University,
earning a B.S. degree in Education with
majors in American History and Sociology.
For some years, she was the Editorial
Director of Reader's Digest Educational
Division. Sally Senzell Isaacs lives in New
Jersey with her husband and two children.

CONTENTS

Peaceful People

The name *Hopi* means peaceful or wise. The Hopi tried to get along peacefully with others groups. In the early 1600s, **settlers** from Spain moved into the area. They built churches and Christian schools. They wanted the Hopi to become Christian and give up their **customs**. Some Spanish people forced the Hopi to work for them.

The Hopi learned to live with the Spanish people. By 1700, the Hopi and Spanish people had become friendly neighbors.

Look for these
The illustration of a Hopi boy and girl shows you the subject of each double-page story in the book.

The illustration of a Hopi dancer highlights panels with facts and figures about daily life in a Hopi village.

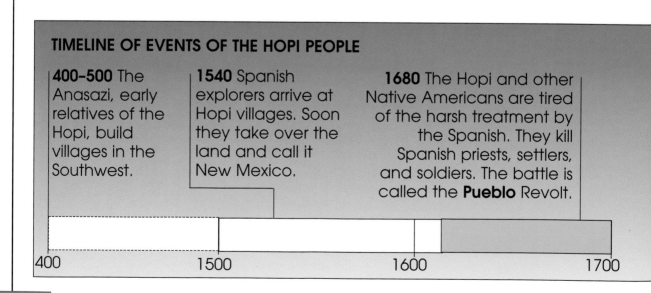

TIMELINE OF EVENTS OF THE HOPI PEOPLE

400–500 The Anasazi, early relatives of the Hopi, build villages in the Southwest.

1540 Spanish explorers arrive at Hopi villages. Soon they take over the land and call it New Mexico.

1680 The Hopi and other Native Americans are tired of the harsh treatment by the Spanish. They kill Spanish priests, settlers, and soldiers. The battle is called the **Pueblo** Revolt.

400   1500   1600   1700

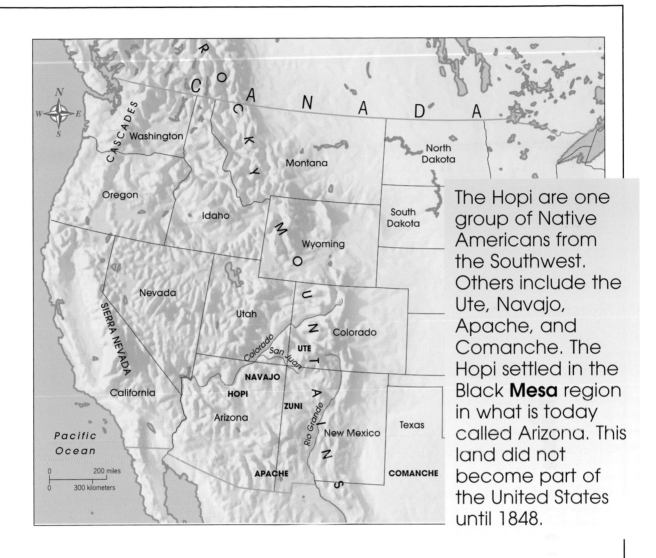

The Hopi are one group of Native Americans from the Southwest. Others include the Ute, Navajo, Apache, and Comanche. The Hopi settled in the Black **Mesa** region in what is today called Arizona. This land did not become part of the United States until 1848.

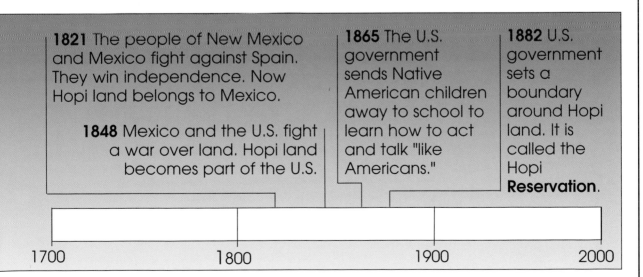

1821 The people of New Mexico and Mexico fight against Spain. They win independence. Now Hopi land belongs to Mexico.

1848 Mexico and the U.S. fight a war over land. Hopi land becomes part of the U.S.

1865 The U.S. government sends Native American children away to school to learn how to act and talk "like Americans."

1882 U.S. government sets a boundary around Hopi land. It is called the Hopi **Reservation**.

1700	1800	1900	2000

A Hopi Village

Arizona is a dry land of sand and stone. It is a land of cliffs and flat mountain tops, called **mesas**. The Hopi used all these things to build their villages. Perhaps the Hopi were looking for safety from the Spanish **settlers** or enemy Native American tribes when they built their villages on top of Black Mesa.

The Hopi live by the Grand Canyon. The land looks the same today as it did thousands of years ago.

About 500 people lived in a village. Their homes were like apartment houses, with rooms stacked above each other. An open area, the **plaza**, was in the center of the village. People gathered there to perform special dances. Special meetings were held in underground rooms called **kivas**.

A village was called a **pueblo**. The walls of a cliff keep this pueblo hidden from enemies.

Hopi Homes

The Hopi built their homes with stones, sand, and mud. The floor of one room was the ceiling of another. A large family of parents, children, grandparents, aunts, uncles, and cousins lived in one building. Women built the houses and owned them.

Inside their homes, there were no beds and chairs. The Hopi sat on blankets or benches. They slept on blankets laid on the floor. They cooked on an indoor fire. Smoke left the house through a hole in the roof.

Hopi climbed ladders to get from one floor to another and to enter homes through a high window.

Hopi pulled their ladders inside at night and felt safe from outsiders.

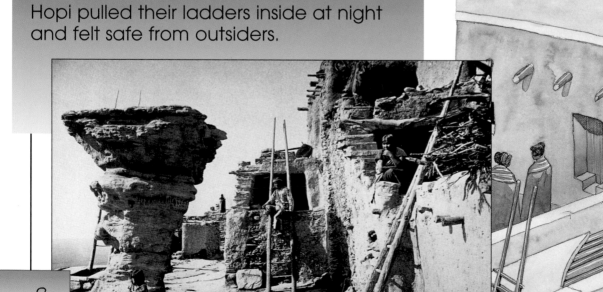

FLOOR BY FLOOR

1st FLOOR: Keep corn, squash, beans, and such special possessions as masks.
2nd and 3rd FLOORS: Eat and sleep; cook in the winter
ROOF: Set fruits and vegetables in the sun to dry; stack fire wood; make pottery; cook in the summer

Families and Clans

When two people got married, they moved in with the wife's parents. Hopi children lived with their parents, grandparents, aunts, uncles, and cousins. This large family was called a **clan**. Every clan had a name, such as the Spider Clan, Snake Clan, and Bear Clan. Many Hopi still live in clans.

Men dressed as **kachina spirits** performed dances from December to June. They wore body paint and masks.

This historical photograph shows young women making a flat bread called piki. They will take it to the houses of the young men they want to marry. If the men eat the piki, they are saying "yes" to the marriage.

Each clan has a special kachina. It is a spirit that helps the people. The spirits cannot be seen. At Hopi ceremonies, men dress like the kachinas and perform special dances. The Hopi believe the dances bring rain, healthy **crops**, and other good things.

Hopi Beliefs

The Hopi believe that **spirits** live in the earth, clouds, mountains, and animals. In the past, the Hopi prayed to the spirits by dancing in the village **plaza**. Sometimes after a dance, the children raced to the fields. They hoped to lead rain clouds to the **crops**.

These Hopi men dance the Snake Dance as a prayer for rain. The dancers hold live snakes.

The **kiva** was the most important place in the village. People climbed down a ladder to this underground room. The Hopi held religious **ceremonies** there. Children were allowed in the kiva after a special ceremony that took place when they were between six and nine years old.

THE FIRST PEOPLE

The Hopi tell stories about the first people on earth. They say people once lived under the ground. They climbed a ladder through a hole in the earth. That hole is in the Grand Canyon.

Some kivas are hundreds of years old. Inside are beautiful paintings.

Working Together

As the sun came up each morning, women took clay pots to the stream. They filled the pots with water for drinking, washing, and cooking. Women spent the day making food, pottery, and baskets. Men headed for the fields to take care of the **crops**.

Women collected wild plants in the desert. They carried them to their villages on their backs in large cloths.

In this photo from 1903, women are making clay pots to be used as water jars, storage bins, cooking pots, and eating bowls.

Each village had a **crier**. The crier brought the news to the people. By climbing on a rooftop and shouting messages, the crier might have announced an upcoming **ceremony** or let people know that planting season was about to begin.

Children

Everyone celebrated the birth of a baby. Relatives and friends gave it a special blanket and an ear of corn, called Mother Corn. The baby and mother stayed indoors for nineteen days. As the sun rose on the twentieth day, the baby was given a name.

Children had many playmates. Their sisters, brothers, and cousins were always nearby.

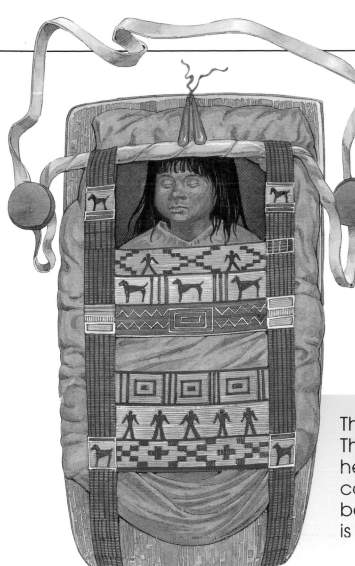

NATURAL NAMES

A Hopi child often is named after something in nature, such as Crow Boy or Little Flower.

This is a cradleboard. The Hopi mother stands her baby inside and carries the baby on her back. The cradleboard is made of animal skin.

Children were free to run through the village, chase butterflies, and play games. Many children played with tops. As tops spun, they made a noise like the wind. The Hopi believed that tops brought windy weather. Parents made children put the tops away in the spring so the wind would not blow the seeds out of the field.

Games

Hopi children played many fun games. The witch game was like Hide-and-Seek. One player, called the witch, took a small drum and hid. The other players had to find the witch. If they could not, the witch beat the drum and ran to another hiding place.

Boys played kickball on open land. Hopi played kickball in the spring because they believed it helped water fill the streams, which was good for their **crops**.

Boys loved kickball racing. Teams of barefoot players spread out for 20 miles (32 kilometers). In each team, one player kicked the ball for a while, then passed it to another. Girls played other games, such as juggling or tossing necklaces over a corncob.

KEEPING WARM

On cold nights, children sat in front of a fire and sang songs. They played clapping games to the tune of the songs.

This Hopi girl is dressed for the Butterfly Dance. The dance celebrates children and the beauty of nature.

Lessons in Life

Hopi children did not go to school. Their parents taught them many things. Girls learned to bake bread and make baskets. They also learned to make ropes from the leaves of plants. Boys learned to grow **crops**, hunt, make tools, and weave cloth.

Children watch their parents perform the Harvest Dance. The Hopi believe the dance will help them get plenty of food from their crops.

Kachina dolls are not toys. They are used to teach Hopi children about the **spirit** world.

As they worked side by side, adults told stories to the children. They explained the history of the **clan**. They taught children to be kind to animals and show respect to older people. Even today, in a ceremony called the Bean Dance, young children learn about **kachinas**, or spirits.

PAINTED DOLLS

Kachina dolls are carved from wood or cactus root. They are painted to represent spirits of the earth, sky, and water. The Hopi still use kachina dolls.

Making Things

The Hopi made everything they needed. They made pottery jars and bowls. They made **wicker** baskets. Women made tools for **grinding** corn and built ovens for baking bread. Men made tools for planting and hunting. They also made blankets, robes, and dancing costumes.

The Hopi use long plant stems to weave wicker baskets and to make flat plaques like this to hang on a wall of a house.

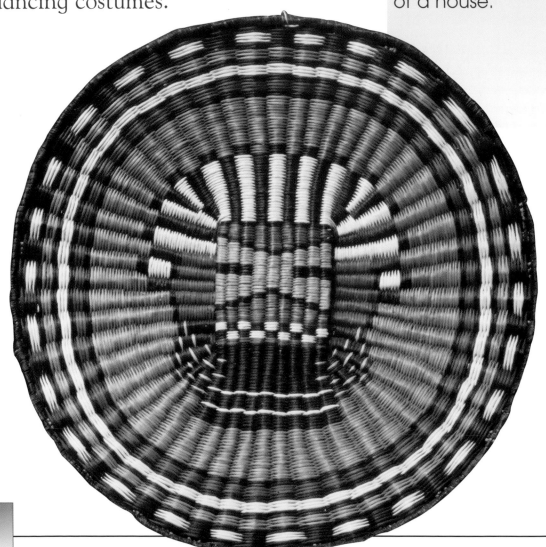

The Hopi have always made beautiful crafts. Hopi people are still making pottery, baskets, and blankets. Many use the black-and-white designs that were used hundreds of years ago. The designs include lightning bolts, clouds, and animals.

USING DEER

The Hopi use all parts of the deer they hunt:
• meat for food
• skins for clothing and drums
• sinew (tissue that connects bones and muscles) for strings on a bow and arrow set
• hoofs for musical rattles

This woman is using wool threads to weave a blanket.

Clothing

The Hopi made their own clothing. Before people from Spain arrived, the Hopi grew cotton. They wore clothing made of cotton cloth. The Spanish people brought sheep to Hopi lands. After that, the Hopi made much of their clothing from sheep's wool.

This teenage girl is getting her hair twisted into two "squash blossoms." Once Hopi girls were married, they wore their hair in braids, like the woman on the left in this photo.

The Hopi made many of their clothes from animal skins. In the summer, men wore only an apron-like skirt. Women wore loose-fitting dresses. In cold weather, they wrapped themselves in blankets. Men and women wore beautiful bead necklaces.

This Hopi man is wearing a bead necklace and a jacket made from deer skins.

Getting Food

Little rain fell on the Hopi's fields. The men dug ditches to bring water from the streams to the fields. This helped them grow corn, beans, squash, pumpkins, and peach trees.

Men dug holes and planted many seeds. They hoped some of the seeds would grow into **crops**. This man is standing in a field of well-grown corn plants.

The Hopi grew twenty-four different kinds of corn. Here are three ears of corn and loose kernels in a Hopi basket.

THE YUCCA

The Hopi found many ways to use the yucca plant. They used the leaves to make sandals, rope, and baskets. From roots and stems, they made soap and shampoo. They ate the yucca fruit.

The Hopi ate more vegetables and fruits than meat. Women walked through the desert and collected wild plants to eat. Nuts, flowers, roots, and stems could be cooked into a fine meal. Not many animals lived in the desert. Still, men and boys sometimes shot deer with bows and arrows. They also trapped rabbits in nets.

Cooking

Corn was part of almost every meal. The Hopi made a crispy flat corn bread and gooey hot cereal. They made corn pancakes that the Spanish called *tortillas*. To make a soup, they cooked corn, beans, squash, and meat in a clay pot over an indoor fire. They baked bread in an outdoor oven.

This Hopi teenage girl is crushing kernels of corn to make flour. The flour is mixed with water to make bread dough. The dough is pressed flat for baking.

Hopi Recipe—Pinole Drink

Pinole is finely ground, sun-dried corn. The Hopi used yellow or blue corn for this recipe. First, they ground the corn into cornmeal. Then they mixed the cornmeal with honey and spices to make a hot, sweet drink.

WARNING: Do not cook anything unless there is an adult to help you. Always ask an adult to help you cook at the stove and to handle hot liquids.

YOU WILL NEED
- 1/2 cup (120 g) yellow or blue cornmeal
- 3 tablespoons honey
- 1 teaspoon cinnamon
- 1 cup (240 ml) boiling water for each person

FOLLOW THE STEPS

1. Heat a frying pan on medium-high heat.
2. Sprinkle the cornmeal into the hot pan.
3. Stir the cornmeal constantly until it turns golden brown (about 8 minutes).

4. When the cornmeal is brown, spoon it into a small bowl.
5. Add honey and cinnamon and stir until it is a sticky paste.
6. Stir one tablespoon of this mix into 1 cup boiling water.

7. Let the liquid sit for 10 minutes. Add more honey if you like a sweeter drink.

You can make three more cups of the drink with the rest of the mix.

Becoming American

In 1848, Hopi land became part of the United States. New railroads brought white settlers to the area. The U.S. government opened schools to teach Hopi children to speak English and to act like White children. Some Hopi were happy with the schools. Others felt they were losing their Hopi ways forever.

HOPI TODAY

Today, about 7,000 Hopi live on **reservations**. These are areas of land set aside by the government. On the reservations, the Hopi try to carry on their traditional beliefs, customs, and ways of life.

Many Hopi live in Arizona today. Hopi colorful costumes and beautiful craftwork continue to be part of American culture.

Glossary

ceremony special way of doing something to mark an occasion, such as a wedding ceremony

clan group of related people

crier a person who calls out loud making announcements or spreading news

crops plants grown to provide food

customs special ways of doing things that have stayed unchanged for many years

grinding crushing, as in grinding corn kernels into a powder

kachinas unseen spirits that help people on earth, represented by the Hopi in dolls and costumes

kiva a large underground room for special meetings and ceremonies

mesa the Spanish word for table; also the flat mountain top where Hopi live

plaza an open space in the center of town

pueblo a Spanish word for a village

reservation land set aside by the government for the use of a particular group of people, such as Native Americans

settlers people who make a new home in a new place

spirit part of a person or animal that holds feelings and thoughts and which cannot be seen or touched

wicker thin stems or branches, often from a willow tree, used to make baskets and furniture

More Books to Read

Sneve, Virginia Driving Hawk *The Hopis.* New York: Holiday House, 1995.

Tomchek, Ann *The Hopi.* Danbury, Conn.: Children's Press, 1998.

Index